PLANT CANDY GATHERINGS

Brandy Cochrane

&

Alexis Skinner

Editor: Chauncey Bellamy
Illustrator: Antonio Clark
Cover Design: Sustainable Initiatives
Front Cover Photo: Solved! Marketing (recipe on page 25)

DEDICATION

To everyone who ever asked, "What do you eat?" this book was inspired by you. Now you get a chance to see what a whole-food, plant-based diet actually looks and tastes like.

–Alexis & Brandy

table of contents.

introduction.

Plant Candy's mission is to celebrate the beauty of fruits and vegetables. Since the summer is ending and the holiday season is beginning, here's a quick guide featuring a few of our favorite plant-based recipes that will be a hit with any group. Our recipes are oil-free, dairy-free, meat-free, and mostly soy-free. We aim for low salt and no added sugars, allowing the fruits, vegetables, and spices to truly shine.

You shouldn't have to journey too far from home to find esoteric ingredients just to make a meal, so we try to choose ingredients that are both simple and accessible, no matter where you cook. Finding fruits and vegetables to eat is easier than you think, and it should be a fun part of your dining experience. Let Plant Candy show you creative ways to hack healthy food by adding more fruits and veggies to your diet, improving your quality of life, and experimenting to make your food fun.

Thanks for supporting the Plant Candy movement. We're excited to make Plant Candy with you!

section 1.
health benefits for
eating a plant-based diet

Black Eyed Pea Soup topped
with mushrooms, caramelized
onions & spinach. Recipe on
plantcandy.com.

Unfortunately, veggies are usually an afterthought, heated up out of a can or a frozen package. Many times, they aren't handled with love and are simply dropped in water or covered with cheese. Because of this, our relationship with vegetables is damaged from an early age. Now let's be clear, Plant Candy isn't trying to convince you to consume plants exclusively. Instead, we encourage you to explore the plant-based foods that are already in your diet, expand on the diverse ways that you can prepare them, and navigate through the unfamiliar plants you've somehow overlooked. Plant Candy recognizes that fruits and vegetables provide a high-density of the vitamins, nutrients, and minerals we need to survive, so it's imperative that we find ways to eat more of them in ways that respect what they bring to the table.

We want to make sure that you're eating a diet that benefits not only animals but also the economy, the environment, and you. Determining what is and what isn't healthy is a real challenge. Every time you turn on the TV or open up a magazine, some expert feeds you a dream that makes what you know is bad for you seem good. Be honest, do you really believe that the "cookie" diet is going to help you lose 40 pounds in two weeks and keep them off? Do you really think that a sprinkle of miracle dust on your food will block all the fat?

We all know that's nonsense, but the global health and diet industry, which is worth over $500 billion, continues to feed us that dream. And we keep taking more bites. With Plant Candy, you don't have to fake the funk anymore. Yes, our recipes are healthy, but they taste great, too. You won't miss the oil, excessive salt, artificial flavors, or foreign chemicals. Instead, you'll be eating well and feeling well, as a result.

Small shifts in your diet can have a surprising impact on your quality of life. Here are some of the benefits of a whole-food, plant-based diet:

Lower cholesterol

High cholesterol levels are one of the risk factors for heart disease, stroke, and peripheral artery disease – the hardening and narrowing of the arteries.

Adding more plants to your diet can help you combat these risks.

"After 4 weeks, the participants eating a plant-based diet, rich in nutrients and phytochemicals, reduced their total and LDL cholesterol significantly more than the participants consuming a standard low-fat diet." – *Stanford Medicine Report, The Effect of a Plant-Based Diet on Plasma Lipids*

Diabetes control

"A team of researchers from the United States and Japan, including the Physicians Committee's Susan Levin, MS, RD and [Neal Barnard, M.D.], published a new meta-analysis showing that a plant-based diet significantly improves diabetes management. A plant-based diet boosts blood sugar control considerably." – *Huffington Post, A Prescription for a Plant-Based Diet Can Help Reverse Diabetes*

Lower risk of heart disease

"'There's no question that diet has a huge impact on heart disease,' says Dr. Walter Willett, professor of epidemiology and nutrition at the Harvard School of Public Health. The study diet features elements that have been closely linked to a lower risk of heart disease: namely, less red meat, less refined starches and sugars, and more fruits and vegetables, says Dr. Willett." –*Harvard Health Publication, Halt heart disease with a plant-based, oil-free diet*

Increased energy levels & Improved digestive system

"Increased energy can be attributed to the addition of more enzymes or minerals that are delivered through plant foods. It is also a result of the energy savings for your body in not having to work as hard during digestive processes, since plant foods are often more easily assimilated by your body." –*Ritual Wellness*

Ongoing detox

"Your body is continuing the process of detoxification because [a plant-based] diet heals the cell membrane, where true detoxification must occur." –Dr.Momonline

Weight control

"Plant-based eating may successfully control weight better than diet pills..." –nutritionfacts.org

section 2.
Useful Ingredients for a Plant-Based Diet

The Plant Candy "Holy Trinity."
jalapeños, onions/scallions & garlic.
Learn more at plantcandy.com.

Now that you're looking beyond putting cheese on your broccoli, pouring oil on your greens, and dumping cups of sugar in your cake batter, whatever will you do? It's a good thing Plant Candy was created by two foodies who refuse to accept the myth that healthy eating is bland, boring, and expensive. Our ultimate goal is to help you improve your relationship with fruits and vegetables. So, here are a few substitutions and enhancements to get you started:

SUBSTITUTIONS	DAIRY	MEAT	OIL	SUGAR	SALT
Beans	x	x	x		
Liquid Amino Acids		x			x
Vinegar			x		x
Vanilla			x		
Cinnamon			x		
Tea		x	x		
Banana	x			x	
Smoke Seasoning		x			
Certain Squashes	x		x	x	
Sweet Potato	x		x	x	

GARLIC

What's this: Garlic is a strong-smelling, pungent-tasting bulb, used in herbal medicine and as a flavoring in cooking. Garlic is pungent when eaten raw.

How to use: It's best enjoyed sliced, crushed, chopped, sautéed, or roasted whole. It's used in savory dishes.

Health Benefits: Treats acne and hair loss, fights the common cold, lowers blood pressure and heart disease risk, and improves bone health.

JALAPEÑO

What's this: Jalapeño is a medium-sized chili pepper used abundantly in Mexican food. Jalapeño is spicy when eaten raw. It loses some of its heat when cooked.

How to use: It's used in savory dishes, both cooked and raw. (Be careful not to touch your eyes while working with this pepper, because its oil will burn them.)

Health Benefits: Relieves migraines, helps prevent cancer, improves the cardiovascular system, prevents sinusitis, relieves congestion, aids weight loss, and reduces inflammation.

CAYENNE & GINGER

What's this: Ginger is a hot fragrant spice made from the rhizome of the plant. Cayenne is a pungent, hot-tasting red powder prepared from dried and ground chili peppers.

How to use: Ginger adds spice without the heat. It can be used dry or fresh. Typically, cayenne is used dry. It offers lingering heat.

Health Benefits: Ginger: Helps reduce nausea, motion sickness, and pain. Cayenne: Relieves upset stomach, intestinal gas, stomach pain, diarrhea, and cramps.

just like meat, vegetables need to be properly seasoned to taste good. If you take a piece of chicken and simply put it in a pan, you probably won't enjoy it. So why expect anything more from vegetables? This chart highlights a few things you can use to add lots of flavor to veggies.

SHALLOTS

What's this: A shallot is a type of onion, but it's sweeter than a typical onion.

How to use: It can be used with onions as a way to add extra flavor to food. It can be dried in the oven, as well. Add it to any savory dish.

Health Benefits: Reduces cholesterol, lowers blood pressure, and is a good source of iron, fiber, potassium, and antioxidants.

What's this: Tea is an aromatic beverage commonly prepared by pouring hot or boiling water over cured leaves.

TEA

How to use: In addition to drinking tea, use it in broths and other cooking liquids to add lots of flavor. For example, Lapsang Souchong tea will add smokey flavors to food with no added fat or calories.

Health Benefits: Strengthens bones, improves digestion, and is a good source of antioxidants.

HUMMUS

What's this: Hummus is a chickpea-based dip used in Levantine and Egyptian dishes.

How to use: It's a good dip for raw vegetables. It can be used in place of mayonnaise on a sandwich or as a spread on bread.

Health Benefits: Lowers cholesterol, balances sugar levels, and is a good source of fiber and antioxidants.

Full Size Chart on plantcandy.com

GREEN COOKWARE

Green pans are safer alternatives to the previous generations of nonstick cookware. They're great for use on the stovetop and in the oven. Just remember to use wooden or other heat-resistant utensils to stir and mix.

SILICONE BAKEWARE

Since silicone bakeware is lightweight and flexible, it increases your storage options. It's an excellent way to keep your treats moist in the absence of oil and dairy. Note that, in certain recipes, lower than normal cooking temperatures and longer than normal baking times may be necessary.

BLENDER

In addition to making soups and sauces, a high-speed blender can make plant-based "ice creams" and pulverize nuts and other ingredients into a fine flour for baking. Some are pricey, so shop smart for a blender that meets your needs.

Here's a range of items that we keep in stock to satisfy all of our plant-based cooking needs. You may already have some of these items, but some of their uses in Plant Candy cooking will surprise you.

PARCHMENT PAPER OR NONSTICK FOIL

These items may be one of the reasons why our dishes come out so well. They help us avoid excessive clean-up, too. All you need to do is measure them out loosely for the pan or dish you're cooking with and fold away the excess. Goodbye, sticky pots and pans!

COOKIE SHEET

A cookie sheet is perfect for both sweet and savory dishes, whether you're roasting veggies, baking donuts, or making our baked falafel. Be sure to pair it with parchment paper or nonstick foil to easily remove food from its surface. Also, have a few handy for large batches.

SIEVE

A sieve can be used in place of a sifter to make flour light and fluffy for baking. It's also useful when creating broths, gravies, and sorbets, and it helps you add flavor from tea leaves to your dishes without having to spoon them out of the finished product. Sieves come in multiple sizes, so you may want to purchase more than one. Either way, make sure you have one with smaller-sized mesh for all-purpose work.

section 3.
The Recipes

Lentil and Quinoa Salad
page 33

Ever wonder why you can't stop eating potato chips? It's because they offer a particular combination of sugars, salts, and fats that keep you going back for more. Now what if you could have the same experience with vegetables, but without the empty calories, clogged arteries, and added pounds? Well, you're in luck, because Plant Candy has found the way. In our kitchens, we experiment with different flavor profiles to find the perfect complements to various fruits and vegetables. We develop tastes and textures to activate your taste buds and satisfy your appetite for flavorful and convenient food. We've created these recipes to both satisfy cravings and offer nutrients that will keep you healthy and your taste buds happy.

section 4.
main dishes

In this section:

Lentil sloppy joe
Lentil Meatballs
Yellow Squash and
Potato Tart

Lentil Sloppy Joe

Time: 1 hour & 40 mins
Yields: 8-10 1/2 cup servings

2 cups dried lentils (16-ounce bag)
4 cups water or vegetable broth
2 tablespoons liquid smoke
1 can tomato paste (6-ounce can)
1 small jalapeño, chopped
4-5 cloves garlic, crushed
1 medium onion, chopped
1 cup diced tomatoes (fresh or canned)
1 ½ cups frozen mixed bell peppers, chopped
1 cup pasta sauce (we use tomato basil)
1½ cups barbecue sauce (we like Sticky Fingers or
Trader Joe's brand)
1 tablespoon dried parsley flakes
2 tablespoons garlic powder
3 tablespoons onion powder
4 tablespoons minced onions
2 teaspoons black pepper

In a pan, soak the lentils in water or broth for 20 minutes.
Turn heat to medium. Add the spices and liquid smoke.
After 20 minutes, when the lentils are slightly tender, stir in
the tomato paste. Add the onions, garlic, jalapeño,
tomatoes, peppers, pasta sauce, and barbecue sauce. Cook
for about 1 hour, until the lentils are fully tender. Serve on
a hamburger bun or over rice or mashed potatoes.

"Meatballs" & Gravy

Time: 55 mins
Yields: About 20 medium sized balls

1 cup dried lentils
2 cups water
1-2 cloves garlic, chopped
1/2 medium red pepper, chopped
1/2 shallot, chopped
1/2 medium onion, chopped
3 sprigs fresh rosemary leaves, chopped
3 sprigs fresh thyme leaves, chopped
1/3 small jalapeño, chopped small
1 tablespoon liquid smoke
2 tablespoons garlic powder
3 tablespoons onion powder
1 tablespoons black pepper
2 slices toast, crumbled into small pieces

Meatballs:

In a pan, add the lentils and water. Cook for 30 minutes over medium heat, until the lentils are tender. (If the water boils out before the lentils are soft, add 1/2 cup of water and cook for an extra 15 minutes.) While the lentils are cooking, chop the garlic, red pepper, shallot, onion, rosemary, thyme, and jalapeño. Mix all of the chopped vegetables together.

Preheat the oven to 350 degrees F. In a pan, without oil, sauté 1/2 of the chopped vegetables. When they begin to stick to the bottom of the pan, add a little water to release them. Stir. Cook until translucent. The peppers should still have a crunch. When the lentils are done, smash 1/2 of them with a fork until they're mealy and crumbled. Add them back to the reserved whole lentils, and mix together. Then, add the cooked veggies, raw veggies, and crumbled toast. Mix together with a spoon or with your hands. If the mixture feels dry, add 1/4 cup of water or broth, a little at a time, to bring the mixture together. Roll into medium-sized balls, and place on a nonstick cookie sheet lined with nonstick foil. Bake in the oven for 25 minutes or until brown. Enjoy with gravy or pasta sauce.

Gravy:

In the same pan used to cook the veggies, add 1 1/2 cups of water and 1/4 cup of soy sauce. Bring to a low boil. Mix 1/4 cup of flour and the remaining 1/2 cup of water, until smooth. Add to the pan. Stir. Finish the gravy with 1/4 cup of white wine. Let thicken.

Yellow Squash & Potato Tart

Time: 1 hour & 15 mins
Yields: 8 sliced or scooped servings

1 bunch scallions
2 pounds potatoes (russet or Yukon Gold), washed and sliced thin
2 medium yellow squash, sliced
1 medium onion, sliced
2 tablespoons garlic powder
1 tablespoon onion powder
1 tablespoon fresh thyme leaves, chopped
1 teaspoon salt
1/2 teaspoon ground black pepper
1/2 cup vegetable broth
1/2 cup nutritional yeast (optional)

Preheat the oven to 375 degrees F. Thinly slice the potatoes, squash, onions, and scallions. Keep separated. Line a pan with nonstick foil. Toss the potatoes and squash with the vegetable broth, garlic powder, onion powder, thyme, salt, and pepper. Layer, in this order, until everything is used: potatoes, onions, squash, then scallions. If you want to use nutritional yeast, sprinkle it on top of the squash between each layer. Bake, covered with foil, for 40 minutes. Uncover, and bake for an additional 25 minutes. Depending on the pan used, cut into wedges or squares to serve.

section 5.
breads

In this section:

Sweet Potato Biscuits
Cornbread

Sweet Potato Biscuits

Time: 40 mins
Yields: About 15 biscuits

2 1/2 cups unbleached flour (plus a reserve)
1 tablespoon baking powder
1/4 teaspoon baking soda
1/2 teaspoon salt
1 cup sweet potato, baked,
cooled, peeled, and blended
1 cup coconut milk (cold)
2 tablespoons apple cider vinegar

Preheat the oven to 425 degrees F. Line a large baking sheet with parchment paper.

"Curdle" your milk by adding apple cider vinegar to it. Set aside for 5 minutes. In a large bowl, whisk flour, baking powder, and salt together. Add the coconut milk and sweet potato to the dry mix, until just combined. If it's too sticky, add more flour. Separate the dough by spooning one dollop at a time. Or, you can cut them uniformly this way: Dust flour on a tray-sized sheet. Roll out, then fold over. Roll out once more. Use a small, shallow bowl or a cookie cutter to shape the biscuits. (You can combine the leftover scraps to shape another whole biscuit, too.) Move the biscuits quickly and carefully to the tray.

Bake for 15 to 18 minutes. Makes about 15 biscuits, depending on the size.

Cornbread

Time: 45 mins
Yields: 8 – 10 pieces depending on pan

1 1/3 cups cornmeal
2/3 cup flour
1/2 cup applesauce
1 cup non-dairy milk
1 teaspoon salt
2 tablespoons vanilla
3 teaspoons baking powder
2 flax "eggs"

For more moisture, add:
1 can blended corn   *   **1/4 cup** non-dairy milk

For flax "eggs":
2 teaspoons flax powder
6 teaspoons cold water

(Mix until gel-like in smallish bowl. Let it sit in the refrigerator for 10 minutes.)

Preheat the oven to 350 degrees F.

In a bowl, combine the cornmeal, flour, baking powder, and salt. Mix in the applesauce, blended corn, flax "eggs," and milk. Place parchment paper in the pan, and pour the mix on top.

Bake for 35 minutes. Let cool.

section 6.
sides

In this section:

Kimchi
Lentil and Quinoa Salad

Kimchi

Time: 15 mins
Yields: 4-5 servings

1 small head of cabbage
3 medium carrots
2 **bunches** green onions
1 large jalapeño
2 **tablespoons** Sriracha sauce
1/2 **cup** rice wine vinegar
1/4 **cup** soy sauce or liquid amino acids
2 **tablespoons** sesame seeds

No cooking required!

Set aside a large plastic bowl. Chop the cabbage finely or into bite-sized pieces. The sooner you plan to eat the dish, the smaller those pieces need to be. Add to the bowl. Do the same with the green onion and jalapeño. Grate the carrots, and mix them with the spices, sesame seeds, and vinegar. Add to the bowl. Add the soy sauce or liquid amino acids. Makes a large batch.

For the best flavor, place the batch in a well-sealed glass or plastic container, and let it sit in a refrigerator for 3 days before serving. It will last about 2 weeks in a refrigerator.

Lentil and Quinoa Salad

Time: 30 mins
Yields: 6 – 8 servings

1 ½ cups whole lentils (any kind), cooked
1/2 cup quinoa, cooked
1 small jalapeño
1 small bunch green onion
1 tablespoon dry mustard
1/2 teaspoon paprika powder
1/2 teaspoon cayenne powder
1/2 teaspoon cumin powder
1/2 teaspoon cracked black pep
1/2 teaspoon celery seed or pov
2/3 cup apple cider vinegar
1 teaspoon liquid smoke

Cook the lentils until just done. Cook the quinoa grains separately. Dice the jalapeño, and slice the green onion. Mix all the ingredients together well. (If you're pressed for time, this recipe can be done in stages: Cook. Refrigerate. Assemble later.) Best served chilled. Yields 6 to 8 servings.

section 7.
desserts

In this section:

Banana Chocolate Chip Cake
Applesauce Spice Cake
Red Wine Chocolate Cake

Banana Chocolate Chip Cake

Time: 1 hour & 30mins
Yields: 6-8 servings

2 cups unbleached flour
2 teaspoons baking powder
1 teaspoon baking soda
1/2 teaspoon salt
1 ½ cups banana (overripe, mashed well)
2 flax "eggs"
2/3 cup date paste (very soft)
1 teaspoon vanilla extract
2 tablespoons apple cider vinegar
1/2 cup cold water
1/2 cup dark chocolate chips (add more or less, as desired)

For date paste:
10-12 dried dates
2/3 cup water

(In a sauce pot with the lid on, add 10 dates and 2/3 cup of water. Bring to a boil, then let sit until the water has cooled to the touch. Pour the water into a blender. Peel the date skins and discard the skins. Add the peeled dates to the water in the blender. Blend to make a paste.)

For flax "eggs":

2 teaspoons *flax powder*

6 teaspoons *cold water*

(Mix until gel-like in smallish bowl. Let it sit in the refrigerator for 10 minutes.)

For maximum time efficiency, preheat the oven to 350 degrees F. Make the flax "eggs," then the date paste. Line a loaf pan with parchment paper. Don't cut the parchment paper precisely, just fold it in at the corners and press upward along the sides of the pan. In a large bowl, stir the dry ingredients (flour, baking powder, baking soda, and salt) quickly with a fork for 1 minute to "sift." Mix in the banana, vanilla, date paste, apple cider vinegar, and water. Be sure to mix well. Add the chocolate chips last.

Pour the mix into the pan, and cover with foil. Bake for 45 to 55 minutes. Let cool for 10 minutes before slicing. Serves 6 to 8.

Applesauce Spice Cake

Time: 1 hour & 30 mins
Yields: 6-8 servings

2 cups unbleached flour
1/3 cup unsweetened cocoa
powder
1 ½ teaspoons baking soda
1/2 teaspoon salt
1 teaspoon cornstarch
1 teaspoon cinnamon
1/4 teaspoon allspice
1/4 teaspoon mace powder
1/4 teaspoon clove powder
1/4 teaspoon nutmeg powder
1 ½ cups applesauce
2 teaspoons vanilla extract
1 teaspoon lemon juice
1/2 cup raisins (add more or less, as desired)

Preheat the oven to 350 degrees F. In one bowl, whisk the dry ingredients together: flour, spice powders, baking soda, cornstarch, and salt. Stir the applesauce, vanilla, and lemon juice into the dry mix, until just blended. Add the raisins last. Pour into a silicone bundt cake mold on a flat tray. Cover with foil. Bake for 45 to 60 minutes. Let cool for 10 minutes before slicing. Serves 6 to 8.

Red Wine Chocolate Cake

Time: 1 hour & 20 mins
Yields: 6-8 servings

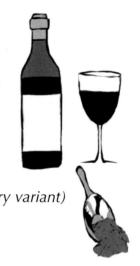

1 ½ cups *unbleached flour*
1/3 cup *unsweetened cocoa powder*
1 teaspoon *baking soda*
1/2 cup *date paste (softened)*
1/2 teaspoon *salt*
1 teaspoon *vanilla extract*
1/2 cup *strawberry jam (or some berry variant)*
1 cup *red wine*

Preheat the oven to 305 degrees F. Yes, 3-0-5 degrees F. In one bowl, sift and combine the flour, cocoa powder, baking soda, and salt. In a blender, on low speed for 1 minute, combine the date paste and berry jam. Use a spatula to scoop the wet mix into a separate bowl. Stir in the wine and vanilla before folding in the dry mix. Pour into a silicone bundt cake mold on a flat tray. Bake for 45 to 50 minutes. Serves 6 to 8.

Plant Candy is committed to helping you improve your relationship with fruits and vegetables without sacrificing taste. Check us out on Instagram @plantcandy, Twitter @plant_candy, and visit our website, www.plantcandy.com, for the latest developments.

Thanks for your support!

We look forward to hearing about your Plant Candy adventures.

Made in the USA
Monee, IL
06 November 2022

17196842R00029